Waves

Joyous and Restless Brimming

Sowmya A.

BlueRose
Publishers
New Delhi • London

First Published in November 2021

ISBN: 978-93-5472-460-2

BLUEROSE PUBLISHERS
www.bluerosepublishers.com
info@bluerosepublishers.com
+91 8882 898 898

Cover Design:
Shreya

Typographic Design:
Namrata Saini

Distributed by: BlueRose, Amazon, Flipkart, Shopclues

Contents

Urban Cocoon 1

Wrath of the Earth 3

Words Stress 5

The Waves of the Sea are Innocent 6

Ogres 7

Empty Pleasures 9

Prayer 10

Living 11

Living Free 12

Aerial Nomad 13

The Journey 14

Home 15

Stolen Hues 16

Haven 17

A Short Love Story 18

Floating Clouds that Promised Rain 19

My Poems 20

Making Sense 21

Drought 22

The Wind Rushed Miles 23

Frozen Ruins 24

Solitude 26

She Told Herself 27

They both were Walking the Same Paths 29

Monsoon Dream on a Summer Afternoon 30

Bushfire 31

Grief-Tipsy 32

Flight 33

Unwinding Memories 34

The Tree with the Face of Buddha 35

Without Much Ado 37

Monsoon Onset 39

Poetry 40

Reflection on Power 42

Spell of the Broken Wings 43

Impasse 45

We are Hiding 46

It's Hard not to Love Air 48

Memories 50

Urban Cocoon

Treadmills wadded in rows
gravely they lay
as metallic tombs of glowing displays
animating ghosts of desires,
ghosts of desired entity,
cocooned in grandiosity.

"Body, mind, and soul loop!"
They advertise on structures similar to coop.
Gliding, sprinting in superhuman pursuit,
altering and pacing to one's strength,
building stamina for a great performance.

Together they whir and whizz, the machines
in unison
amidst low puffs
as when ships swarm the rippling tides
voyaging in woodenly silences.
Sailors in search of promising lands
navigate the charted map of possibilities.

Eyes gleaming in toil,
bodies sweating out hopes,
they march in crammed tropes.
Like hunters, food gatherers
they get ready for a battle!

To chisel the contours of a fleshy race on a
bandwagon.

Like sleep walkers
they move to and fro.
Or like a trapped fly knocking windshield,
they linger in predictable tempos and awkward
repetitions.

Each as a floating island,
self-absorbed, meeting other eyes in furtive glances
in compound mirrors of many panels.
Each to his own and her own
sees the clefted views in glorifying images
reflecting capital logos
on shoes and bottles,
on bodies and smirks,
living the dreams of the urban surplus.

Wrath of the Earth

The Earth, the sphere of life,
Mother, sustaining zillions of lives,
is now fragmented into blocks and sold by square feet.
Civilization means burying it with skyscrapers, granites
and concrete.
Splendid hills are carved, mined, distorted,
and blotted with spots of tall towers.

The fragile hills and valleys,
do they ever crumble?
Turning these arrogant structures upside down?
Giant machines dig deep causing trenchant wounds.
As fractal, chaotic patterns of smoke rise,
the clouded sky looks down in sheer dismay.
Everywhere the Orb bears a cursed look by greed's
ominous touch.
Its lustful breath vying for destruction, possession, and
obliteration.

The puny beings are always shaken off their
 smug power.
The planet has its own way of getting back with
appropriate reply.
The mighty mound of life is yet to straighten out its
crumpled creases of aches
and devour all with its centrifugal force.

The wrath of the Earth…
Would we escape the inescapable?
Would we redeem ourselves at all?

Words Stress

Words drop at dead end sometimes.
Traversing unfathomable depths
or swivelling in inglorious shallowness,
nothing can supersede a person
as these proxy supplants!

Meanings stretch and quibble
into the oblivion of known or unknown shores.
They swell and dwell
in happy or unhappy thoughts,
both in sullen or graceful composures.
They grade, upgrade or degrade
each to its own capacity.
They tweak, they squeak
sometimes more is less and less is more.

Silence, its estranged mate,
rebuffs its talkative course
and sermons with a smirk,
"With the weight of 'I', 'You', and the 'World'
you always incline an uphill road.
Better mind, folks rate me above you,
You, for their excesses, and I, for their peace"

The Waves of the Sea are Innocent

The waves of the sea are innocent
frothing, juggling back and forth
in restless agony and joyous brimming.
Agony capped by movement
joy shadowed in the monotony of rippling tides.

They know not why they move at all…
In rhythmic grace and tumultuous haste
waves rush in and rush out,
to touch the face of the Earth,
to tickle the beach,
to linger on its memory for a brief while
with a soft splash they recede back further and further
as if reminded of their role in the middle of the ocean.

The cool, calm and gentle Earth
glistens momentarily in the lingering memory of the
waves,
soaking in happy thought!
The waves just want to come and go
without the tedium of formality,
without the rituals of rendering reasons for their visits.
The waves just want to gaze at its gleeful, platonic pal.
And may be for nothing else…

Ogres

Tiny feet struts the savage patch of land of withering
grass
half-dancing, half-leaping.
Nature itself would join in the ecstatic dance of
innocence.
Laugh rolls out like the babbling of slender yet hasty
moving waterfall.
Melody, music enough to kindle sprouts of green in the
barren land,
tender enough to tranquilize the sternest of the stern.
The solace, hope, and song of humanity -- the tender
lives.

Unused to the heaving, rhythmic and artistic walk of
the grownups
little babe, micro-image of femininity, walks the strides
of joy
unmindful of fatal insects, cunning hyenas and
merciless carnivores.

Watching with the foxy, naked eyes
he grips his prey in wanton cruelty
shredding the tiny bud of life
with meditated bestiality, hardened criminality,
stubbing out cigarette on translucent budding leaf.

Has the world exhausted its stock of tenderness?
Has the age become sick to devour its younger ones?
Are we still humane or have we turned into deranged
ogres?

Empty Pleasures

Eyes open in a hurricane of ambitions;
desire to get more, buy more, and fill more.
When walking through countless malls and bazaars,
wish to be more, stock more, fills up
in an eagerness to buy the whole planet!

Desire, a word that rings numerous meanings in
everyone
A Circle entwined in heaps of circles
Circle never yielding calm
touching the surface of it we swim aimlessly
getting entangled in more circles.

Determination, courage, and will power all for fake
reasons.
Journey for material goals is what all crave for.
Journey towards the inward is what is seldom cared
for.

Prayer

Tardy, slow, sparse rain visits the stifling planet
like an unwilling guest
bestowing a trifle favour to the rival.
Drought prays to the affected visitor
in selfless earnestness,
"Drench deep the stiffened logs,
ghost-looking trees, the parched Earth.
Pierce as long needles,
Hammer the cracked soil with ferocious force,
Spear into the weedy rhizomes,
Cane the unmoving smudges of summer's horrors,
Soak the hardened soil,
Sprout the tender translucent emerald."

Living

Some flowers flash and fade.
Some bloom and linger on for days.
Few are through months.
They all germinate.
Luckiest of them lived and borne all:
Memories of the sun and the moon,
of rains and droughts,
of bees and pests,
of rainbows and storms,
of breezes and floods
of wildfires and stars.

Living Free

The flowers bloom not in total neediness of the Spring.
They blossom for the sky.
They cheer for the wind,
for the rain,
for the soil,
and of all, they are happy for themselves.

Aerial Nomad

The sailor of the air glides and floats
flashing its airfoil palette
blotching hues on the green canvas.
Its past, a painful memory;
its future, a fleeting dream.

Dreamy, it floats on happy wings
unfettered by past or future.
The lost dreamer, an acute sensor of the Earth's
pulsation,
notches the heavy air with a subtle knowledge
unknown to the rest.
Steady in its fragile strides, leaps across time.

Saint or a happy-go-lucky fool?
The probes may mean nothing,
non-existential for the butterfly.
In the meantime, the mind captures the flash of the
fairy dream
and revels in its soft flaps of joy.

The Journey

The deserted lanes of that unknown town
reminded nothing of the purposed journey.
The address was lost.
The host had become a faint memory.

Home

When the night draped a dark pall vaporizing the last
bright shoots,
a hatchling turtle was finding home from grassroots.

It moves dazed,
toeing wild,
as a helpless child,
totally beguiled.

Navigating its way through a dark sandy passage
pacing mirth
on a way faintly lit by the hanging moon and stars,
it treads the sandy crust of the magnetic earth
to meet its cradle of crystalline waters.

Stolen Hues

A droplet hurrying down a misty firmament
slid off, landing on a flower.
Dazed by a riotous colour,
it let in the hues into its vacant sphere.

Mired in the hazy dream of the flower
it flashed, hiding behind a shadowy dream.

The rushing wind popped the dew into minuscule of
vapours
in one effortless sweep of grace
wiped off the drop and its trace
vanishing both the dew and its stolen hues.

Haven

Like springs jolting brittle woods
splaying random hues
into the summer-burnt canvas,
as migrant birds glide high airs searching for safe
havens,
like a tempest-haunted ship returning to its dock,
and as turtle hatchlings toe back to their watery
home...

With the sharpness of the pendulum clock,
with the precision of the Newton's Cradle,
with the ease of optimism,
with the turmoil of scepticism…

My thoughts find you over and over
and I return to your groove.

A Short Love Story

Ripening light of the setting Sun
turns bare walls into a live canvas.
Colours to dispel the gloom?
or shadows to cast after shafts of lustre?

The Sun dips into oblivion,
traces of shine recede the walls.
Poised eve moved on
detached to the fleeting moment of exhilaration.

Floating Clouds that Promised Rain

A shallow film of white clouds cluster,
as a canopy to the sweltering day.
Untimely twilight lulls a hazy dream of rain.

But clouds stay an unmoved portrait;
grey and silver.
It almost rained without drops of rain.
Like a soulful rendition choked by a half-hearted
impulse.

My Poems

Words strewn in short lines
struggle to follow long trails
of mind's complex bytes.

Words, I call as poems,
give tiny patterns to my unknown fears,
sets readable tempo to stupefying ideas,
like an old song long-forgotten
suddenly remembered
syncing with the current situation
helps to make sense of the mess.

Making Sense

Butterfly flapping its wings
may be a sign of a racing heart or imminent tornados.
No devastation in nature has the history of being
'deactivated'
after someone who studied it predicted.
Theories remain scientific assumptions
just as some sacredly believed myths.

Everything boils down to one existential question:
Can lives be saved and occurrences understood, if
truths of world are discerned?

A bird sensing gale
flies away instinctively
deserting its nest on tree
The bird, saved, cannot brag about its "sixth sense."
It can only grieve for the nest and its habitat
as a story in human language, that could make sense,
stays behind unable to reach the bird.

Drought

Clouds draped Sky lingers on choked.
Glaciers hoarded in its vapoury void.
The Earth, still in summer shock, plays a cold host,
stays stolid.

The Wind Rushed Miles

The wind rushed miles to catch up on a rainbow
stretching bowed.
Missed a yellow field;
a sunset, skipped.
a gurgling waterfall nearby,
a pasture too went by,
all trivial stints ignored in the sprint.

Though, it had left.
The rainbow, spotless bright,
had melted into the sky spread in pitch-dark hues.

Backward journey was long -
as it was told by a few bruises.

Frozen Ruins

The roads spell one to go on in rehearsed pace.
The inner map hitch and hijack
stored memories
boxed and lost in recess of dark valleys.

Valleys were lost too, in no time,
when connect bridges crumbled,
thinned day by day.
Ropes withered
and the light from the last house in the town faded as
the wagon moved away into a dazzling city of
thousand lamps.

Where were these roads?
lost in valleys
and lost valleys...
Where was this guiding map?
In the debris of crumbled bridges?
Recovered and readable, every word of it!
or are only the recovered words, legible?
the rest eluded in valleys of lost valleys?

Genie's lamp rubbed! And the magic begins!
Unfolding in the inner scope were things:
things you remembered,
names you knew,
landmarks you have not forgotten
trick you to believe in disbelief
things that are not,
things that are,

as you believed!

Roads, layered in few wrinkled layers
tar, gravel, stones loaded in thin heaps
on a ruddy muddy paths that
disappeared in monsoon,
cleared in summer.

Big temple then,
a humble structure now,
shyly covering its half-worn paint.
Town that once threatened to throw you
into an abyss of chaos with people, noise and buzz,
looks tamed with the grace of an 80-year-old.
Its older streets are narrower, still.
Houses have before them different patterns of rangoli,
old mopeds and some faint signs of change.

The streets resemble those who chose to stay:
ageing and thoughtful.
Some houses are locked and in ruins.
Those were of the ones who chose to leave.
Extension colonies on fringes, on receding farm lands
are the grandkids!
Thriving and growing - hale and hearty
in offbeat haste.

Grand and trivial details once remembered and
connected
are now elusive to grasp.
With twenty five years behind
it's hard to say -
If retrieval of the lost track was helped by the frozen
town or by the frozen memories?

Solitude

To travel alone the untrodden tracks,
to feel the tremors of quivering spirits,
to hear the pulsation of thumping beats,
to sense seconds in splits.

To be at the edge of a slope -- scariest,
facing down the valleys -- steepest,

to be sinking down in waters -- deepest.
to walk in forest - darkest
totally at the danger's behest;

To come back from a cliff -- graver,
to swim back to a shore -- safer,
to be found by another lost wanderer
is the artistry of the 'lost trail'.

The trail where calamity precedes serenity and
prudence completes solitude.

She Told Herself

She told herself that it's a fool's dream,
slipping grains of sand through fingers,
insanity leading her to the brink of death.

She told herself that she was chasing rainbows,
a dream that would sap her last drop of life,
twist and tweak her soul like a chocolate wrapper,
and she won't ever get it in the way she aspired.

She told herself that no good will ever come clinging
on to it,
sand castle on sandy beach won't last,
and that she won't find her shell lost in the ocean,
again.

She told herself to forget of all its enchanting
memories,
that would take her to the peak of unconditional
feelings,
unhinged tenderness
and into the depths of pure stream of reflections.

So she told herself that life can be better,
with better days,
without her dream!
without her being in the dream!!

Surging fears transmuted
as gagged feelings,
and they told her
in their silent eloquence,
that they are alien to the language she speaks.
The roots and the cords they emerged through do not
speak the same language as her.

They both were Walking the Same Paths

She was smitten by the forests' charm
aware of all that could harm,
in a surreal quest to live.
He searched in it for a thing he has no name to give.
Lost were they in their own pursuits.
Both tread the traps of slippery tracks
sans lights or knacks.

Two paths crossed in a quasi-reunion,
colliding with each other head-on.
Face-to-face they stood
seeing the symmetrical features of shared pasts,
of lost dreams, and shared grief reflected in
each other's eyes
tell- tale of losses and failures,
and faint signs of hopes shining in the gazers.

Confided they with each other
the bits of their jigsaw puzzles
trying to find missing pieces for each other's lives.
The linear stories converged
with sobs, joys and hopes.

Their journeys were not in vain.
sadness of meeting the same fate
was a little bargain
made in an attempt to sustain
a vanishing gain.

Monsoon Dream on a Summer Afternoon

Downpour in an autumn charred afternoon,
melting under the scorching sun
hung on with vapours of descended drops.
The drops danced hard in passionate rhythm,
the day gleamed in surreal spell.
The fogged vista cajoled the faintly passing out day's
moments
with Monsoon dreams.

The untimely rain blew fresh breaths
de-staining layers and layers of frozen cells.
New growth, fresh tints, suspected.
Dews on quivering foliage adorned
as a deluding charm to the scorned.
The rain ended; with it, the hazy magic.
Drop by drop they receded;
Some drained, some became soil, and some
disappeared without trace.
Piercing the thinning clouds,
the Sun re-emerged
dousing the vapour blanket.
drop by drop.
With it, the untimely Monsoon dream too dripped,
rapidly.

Bushfire

All was melted,
charred, contorted.
All that animated it once -
untamed forests, beings of the wild.
Murky abyss, it turned
from a sanctuary of a rare kind.

A true tryst it was,
of nature and fervour!
For the Earth, at least!

The bushfire saw no value in those living trophies,
seen as trifles and worthless,
it took them all in bouncing flames, in hostile embrace.

Like the charred remnants of dead things on the
blackened earth,
memories hung on as ungracious souvenirs.

Yet, the bushfire failed to sway
the obstinate Earth's might to sprout green again,
naivete' to harbour and love
all that had scorched it before.

Grief-Tipsy

Lines written in an inebriated sadness
are hard to make sense of
by the sober in their sobriety.

Flight

Feisty rain that fell hard
hopped on its monsoon winds and retracted slowly.

not in dejection
not in rejection.

It feared the approaching winter
would freeze the droplets
and leave them hanging as icicles on a windowsill.

Unwinding Memories

In a moment of void,
gyrating movement of a cormorant's wings
unleash a train of happy thoughts
in chaotic tempo.

Memories in the deeper pool
are sifted
as a duck that dives its head to sift water.

The Tree with the Face of Buddha

Gobs of lush branches floated over
against a vast blue cover.
The tree stood like the Earth's emerald ornament
elegant and natural in its own locus by the curve of a
pavement;
the banyan with clumps of aerial roots.

Buzzing wings lived amidst rustling leaves.
All through days and nights
dreams chirped for the tree; animated its set self
in the racket of honks and
whirs of angry wheels.

Block - it was seen as
by the restless movers,
a distraction for the listless crowd.
So it was put down
with a chain saw.

Layers on the surface of a mutilated tree
narrated years of patient growth.
Now a chunk, a bald spot.

Random hands coloured it
with the face of a smiling Buddha.
He mused on a dismal tree
sticking to its bark.

Tiny shoots of leaves sprouted
from the corners of his dreamy eyes.
The aching tree stripped of all its bulk
stayed solemn for the return of the buzzing wings,
once more.

Without Much Ado

Far away, a mining land rumbles with a sinking boom,
raising a colossal debris in the loam.

Leaving still waters in ripples;
hearts, with skipped beats.

In a distance, an engine's squeals ebb and flow
on roads that bear beatitude glow.

Meters away, a concrete mixer runs
quivering chairs, desks, and benches.

Feet away, two people enter into a brawl
sound-splashing corridor and wall.

Classrooms heave regular noises
in rhythmic fall and rise.

A class goes mute
after papers ruffle quick and soft.

They write test
with hands speeding, heads bent.

A sparrow darts into a still class
manoeuvring its head many degrees.

Out it goes with a dormant spider
wings ruffling, receding quicker.

A line of ants on busy queues
gather the arachnid's broken, weightless remains.

And march they do,
without much ado.

Monsoon Onset

Roads, deserted, emanating tiresome hot smoke from
cracked, chapped earth
lay like wounded animals, unmoved.
Winds are burnt, hot, and heavy.
They move in maimed movements.
Reluctant, trapped under trees, tied to towers, swirling
in small motions.
They drag their invisible selves hither thither.
Day is torched with hundred suns lashing.
The Earth is resilient with battered patience.
Its tolerance still wicking last of the flames
burns on steadily protected by the unseen protective
hands.

A mystical shadow comes between
the burning Sun and the sweltering earth.
A white aura canopies,
heavy drops of rain come down in divine chastisement
lifting the dusty crust of the emerald,
shining it in vibrant hues.
Struggling winds are set free like thousand genies to
work on each inch with magical touch
sprouting seeds, fruits and buds of flowers.

Poetry

Between the impulse to talk and to silence my
thoughts,
now I choose the latter.
In silence, I reach for my close friend these days.
This friend and I get along too well
I don't speak to him often
and when I finally choose to say a few things to him,
he is glad.
He is only too glad to listen,
and I couldn't be gladder.

Our meetings spread out on a half-moist earth
thrilled by the shy rain stopped halfway.
He is all dazed and ears
amused at my juvenile attempts to string words.
He offers me endless chances to say things I want to,
correct, edit, and rephrase any part.
Smiling, he would let me delete and edit.
For him, none of what I say is exaggeration
None of my feelings, too strong.
He offers me the whole world of words
to select and make mine.
When I weave an image for him, he blushes.
When I use rhythm, he smiles.
He has all the time when I reach him
He won't make me jealous,

and has eyes, only for me!
My best friend of all...
If he were human, he would let me say all to him.
Keeping me away from my best friend!

Reflection on Power

History teaches us the powerful are the most
dangerous.
They meditate, scheme, use their power and strike.
When predators attack in measured intelligence,
the attack is laced with heartless vigour, beastly glory,
and distracting meditation.

A puny sparrow with its whizzing wings dashes in
darting its head in confused streaks.
It rotates its little head with its small beak
shuffling hither and thither in confused mono actions,
searches hesitantly in corners of the roof for spider
webs and spiders,
flies towards the target with petrified anxiety in many
suspended attempts,
beaks the spider in slow but quick motion,
heads out with its head,
stuck in its tiny beak.

Spell of the Broken Wings

A warm March afternoon's still breeze
shored up a weightless wing of a Monarch
and laid it softly on drab leaves.
A tiny strip of the Monarch,
glowed as an erupting sliver of lava,
in the camouflage of lifeless bed of dried foliage.

Within a meter's distance other pieces of wings lay
scattered
as mixed up pairs of earrings
kept for sale in an art mela.
The strips of wings
as an enchantress, dissipating
the predilection for normal,
conjured up a spell of the broken.

The spell fixing up the scattered figments,
was composing unwritten notes of odes on 'the
broken,' yet intact.
The broken pieces of the wings were
bringing back the image of the butterfly together
binding them with melted strands of gold.

Did the winged beauty get into a wild fight?
Or rushed in tumult towards its abode?
Dropped its wings and forgot about them?
Or left them on purpose, as a sign?

Where did the limb of a wingless butterfly go?
The butterfly, which lapped and flapped,
on the lap of many flowers...
Does it crawl now in the corporeal conundrum?
Or walk amidst the green ambush?
Does the absence of pain receptors make it angelic...
Or having wings make it invulnerable to pain...
Now that it is wingless,
Does it still not feel the pain?
Does it remain non-reactive even to the memory of its
metamorphosis?

The questions lingering in the liminal human
experience
lead nowhere as the wings float and vanish on a cart-
less chariot.

Impasse

Once,
words trailed
as easily and cozily
as the buzzing wings to
blossoming galore of fruit laden woods.

Euphony of sounds and colours.

Now
words elude...
scattered thoughts scarecrow
exotic birds
making them fly across borders.

Empty nests...

bird tracks on drying river beds
and
a few littered words
lay like last feathers of flown birds.

We are Hiding

We are holding on to our lives
We are seeking puddles of hopes, peace, and pleasure.
Turned hedonistic by the virulent times
in uncertainty of life,
in expectancy of imminent threat.
And they call us covid warriors.

We now look at our front yard
and regret not planting trees.
We admire the frontline warriors
and fumble in our little spaces.
We muddle through movies, news and jokes
talk about some stories and muffle some
looking for truths through screens
of all sizes.
We watch some and skip some
depending upon our moods.
Choosing to believe what the virtual world says
sliding it through our finger,
mostly going by what media dictates
as a thumb rule.

We sometimes huddle together for Netflix and Prime
with social distance intact,
sharing passwords
and logging in our personal devices.

We worry about food, education,
and vaccines
talking about them over and over in our little
comforts.
When the globe is battling the pandemic,
We, privileged to be in lockdown,
do our bit inside the house.
And they tell us,
"You too are covid warriors."

It's Hard not to Love Air

Fire burns on to leave its ashy trail,
passion is the name given to it.
Blazing both self and others in alchemy,
divine purity? Carnal rage?
Capricious, it can be and unpredictable,
beauty in flames and smouldering mysticism.

Earth loves and gives all...
Like mother, it sustains and bears all.
The essence of all existence is coloured by the grace of
this majestic bounty.

Ether, the inexplicable jargon,
a luxury for beings' cave-living instincts.
An encompassing compass for all expediential souls!

Uttering this name would cure and raise thirst!
Water --- the name is a cool word drop.
Antidote for the Earth's all maladies.
a potent element balancing Fire and Ether.

Air! a perfect lover!
In every breath, till death!
Never trumpets its presence.
But it's there in all times of need.

It rests in us like smiles and tears.
Nowhere to be seen but call on as and when to suit the moods,
from an enchanting breeze to a forceful storm,
from wind to a tornado,
its every vista, loveable to the core.
Omnipresent, it knows each life.
Honest trickster, it moves in sneaky bouts and sincere norms.
Absorbed sometimes,
but knows how to disentangle.
Transcends all limits
from being entity to no entity.

Memories

Memories splatter over my window pane
as drops of rain.
I smile...
At their sincerity,
at their eagerness,
to bring with them
shells from memories' shores,
each time they visit.